Thinking Styles®

Relationsh _____ es
that _____

Fiona Beddoes-Jones

BJA Associates Ltd

The author can be contacted at BJA Associates Ltd, Stainby, Lincolnshire, NG33 5QT, UK

E-mail: *author@thinkingstyles.co.uk*
Web site: *www.thinkingstyles.co.uk*

Thinking Styles® is a registered trade mark.

Papers used by BJA Associates Ltd are natural, recyclable products made from wood grown in managed and sustainable forests. This forms part of BJA Associates' environment policy.
Printed and bound in Wales by WBC Book Manufacturers.
Production by The Maverick Team, PO Box 5555, Newark, Nottingham.
Cartoons and Illustrations by Sarah Nelson, mobile number 0378 268929.
The 'Philbert in the City' cartoons contained in this book are copyright to BJA Associates Ltd, 1999.
BJA Associates Limited Reg. No. 3444947
ISBN 0 9535310 0 7

For all of you who think like me,
and for all of you who don't.

Especially my husband, Nick.

Acknowledgements

I have often wondered, were we to make different choices in our lives, if, spiritually, we would still arrive at the same 'place' at the same 'time'. Assuming, of course, that wherever we are at a given time is where we are meant to 'be'! A philosophical introduction with what is, probably, an impossible question to answer. However, it does lead me onto the acknowledgements for this book:

Some years ago I met an international business consultant, Franz Venter, who introduced me to the work of one of the gurus of thinking skills, Edward de Bono. Little did I imagine then that, fifteen years later, I too would be writing a book on thinking. It was also because of Franz that I entered the world of management consultancy, where I met my husband, Nick.

Therefore special thanks are due to Franz, wherever in the world he may be, to thank him for setting me on the path that I now tread. I am eternally grateful that we met.

No book is ever written by its author alone and this book is certainly no exception. Heartfelt thanks go to my editor, Julia Miller, for her flexibility and attention to detail, David Bowman of AA Books, and to those friends, clients and colleagues who have kindly reviewed the book for their advice, patience and generosity of spirit.

I would also like to thank the staff of WDP for their continued support of the Thinking Styles project. Then lastly, and perhaps most importantly, a huge debt of gratitude is owed to my wonderful husband, Nick, who has supported me and our family during the development and writing of Thinking Styles, and never wavered in his belief that Thinking Styles would be a success.

Fiona Beddoes-Jones, 1999

Contents

1   Introduction

Welcome to the first in the series of the Thinking Styles books. I really ought to begin by explaining why I initially developed Thinking Styles, the purpose of this first book and why I call it 'Relationship Strategies that Work'.

I met my future husband at work and we made a very good team, however, I found it fascinating that we seemed to think in completely opposite directions. I am sure many couples and partnerships will know exactly what I mean, and this was, by turn, either very interesting, very funny or very frustrating! I have always had an interest in people, and when we decided to marry I began my research into the ways in which the brain works and how people learn through thought, behaviour and language. Fairly quickly I realized that, 'I was on to something'.

I couldn't find a questionnaire or diagnostic tool which accurately measured 'thinking' in the way in which I understood it, or in a way which was easy for a layperson to understand. Knowing how useful it had been for myself and my husband to be able to communicate more effectively by being able to 'talk each other's language', I began work on Thinking Styles in 1996.

Thinking Styles is marketed by BJA Associates Limited.

The company's mission is:

to contribute to society by assisting individuals, teams and organizations to build better relationships through understanding themselves and others more fully.

This book is designed to do just that and by investing your time in reading it you are helping BJA Associates and myself to achieve that mission, for which I thank you.

Thinking Styles consists of a questionnaire and report which identifies people's preferences and flexibility in their thinking skills. There are no 'right' or 'wrong' answers. Each of us is an individual, unique in our own way. That we can grow and develop by learning new things or by building on what we already know, is one of the wonderful things about being human.

How to Use This Book
This book is a pragmatic approach to thinking styles and is not intended to be an academic work. How you decide to read the book will depend very much on your own thinking style. Some of you will start at the beginning and work through to the end, others of you will dip into those chapters which particularly attract your attention. Assuming that, ultimately, you will read the whole book, both ways will be equally as effective. You may also find that as you read it for a second or third time, you notice things that you missed before.

I have deliberately written Thinking Styles without the use of academic language or jargon. This may disappoint those of you with a preference for jargon or complexity, but will doubtless be a huge relief to everyone else! And although I do not pretend to have identified all of the 'thinking styles' we, as human beings, use on an almost daily basis, I am glad that, in my own way, I have at least made a start by bringing the twenty-two thinking styles explained in this book into people's conscious awareness.

If you are one of those people who likes to flick through a book before you read it, you may have already noticed 'Philbert', our cartoon character. Philbert works for Green, Grow & Ethics, a city firm of ethics consultants. He is recently married and loves his wife although he doesn't pretend to understand her. He enjoys his job and has a lot of fun at work with his colleagues, particularly because he often doesn't understand them either. Many of the cartoons are based on real people and real events, so, as you read through the chapters, you might find yourself laughing and thinking 'I know that person!'

To give you a summary of the issues and some hints and tips to help you at work, I have included a short section on Management and Motivation for each thinking style. It briefly explains how to manage or motivate someone with that style and, if they are your manager, how best to approach them and present them with your work or ideas.

If you decide that you would like to develop more flexibility regarding your thinking skills, I have also included in each chapter some exercises for you to complete in your own time.

At the end of each chapter you have the opportunity to estimate a score for your own preferences. The 'easiest' way to do this is to read the summary boxes at the end, and, according to how many summary points you tick as applying to you, give yourself a percentage score for that style. For example, if you tick four out of six summary points, give yourself a score of 67%, which would be 'Moderate'. Mark your preferences with a dot and then join them together as shown below. A 'low' score is below 35%, and a 'high' score above 70%.

If you have no preference for one of the styles and have not ticked any of the summary points, give yourself a zero score for that style. Your line will therefore begin from zero. The styles are not mutually exclusive and although you may have a strong preference for some of the styles, it is equally possible that you will have natural flexibility for them all.

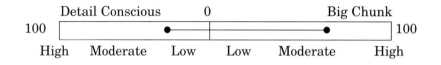

I hope that this will be the kind of useful little book that you will want to give to your friends, colleagues, partners, bosses, employees and children. And I sincerely hope that reading this book and learning about thinking styles will enhance the quality of *all* your relationships.

$\mathcal{2}$ **Background**

The thinking styles I write about in this book have not been 'invented' by me. This becomes particularly obvious when you read some of the quotes contained in the various chapters from the ancient Greeks and Romans! What I have done is write about these particular thinking styles in a way which is easy for people to read, understand and apply to their own working lives.

Much of what I have included in this book is based on the work of Lesley Cameron Bandler and Richard Bandler from the early 1970s in America in the area of personal therapy. They did not talk about 'thinking'; instead they used the terms 'fundamental filters' and 'meta-programmes' to explain ways in which people perceive and understand the world around them and how they then translate that perception of the external world into an internal representation in their own minds. The Bandlers' work is recognized as some of the first building blocks of Neuro Linguistic Programming (NLP). If, after reading this book, you are interested in learning more about NLP, you will find a list of recommended books and web site addresses in Chapter 22.

Have you ever wondered why there are some people you can talk to and understand easily, and yet there are others you find more difficult to comprehend? It is quite likely that those 'difficult' people process information in a different way from you, something that I am sure both you and they find equally frustrating!

Thinking Styles is divided into a number of Sensory Criteria and Other Criteria, making a total of twenty-two individual thinking styles. Each style is accompanied by particular behaviours and language patterns, many of which I have identified in the chapters. This makes the styles easy to identify with skill and practice, although I would urge you not to underestimate the amount of skill and practice that it takes to identify them easily.

By learning about the thinking styles and their associated language patterns and behaviours, you can achieve the following benefits:

- increased understanding of yourself and others
- improved relationships with friends, colleagues and partners
- avoidance of conflicts at work and at home
- prevention of misunderstandings
- minimization of disagreements
- more effective motivation of others
- improvement in teamwork and group dynamics
- increased impact and effectiveness of communications
- saving time and money

The Thinking Styles programme can also generate a Two-Way Relationship Profile, where two individuals' preferences are compared and contrasted, overlaid one on to the other. This is a very useful way to understand how two people's thinking may either conflict with, or complement, each other.

Groups and teams have found the Thinking Styles Profile particularly helpful. By understanding the group's individual and collective thinking preferences two things happen:

- individuals are valued and treated with more respect
- the team becomes stronger and more cohesive as a result

There are no 'right' or 'wrong' answers regarding thinking styles, only personal preferences in how your brain naturally processes information, and it is important to remember this. Thinking Styles has been designed to identify thinking preferences and your flexibility of thinking. Thinking Styles does *not* measure your thinking ability nor is it a measure of intelligence.

I would add that some thinking styles preferences are more appropriate for some job roles in certain circumstances. For example, if you were buying the house of your dreams, would you want a solicitor with a big chunk, strategic processing preference or would you want the most detail conscious person you could find?

The descriptions of behaviour I have given for each thinking style describe an extreme preference for that style. The degree to which the behaviours are true will be different for each of you, even though there will be similarities. So, do not expect all the examples given to be directly relevant to you.

Remember also that the scores you give yourself will reflect that moment in time and, should your circumstances alter, so too might your preferences and scores.

(Please note that the example profiles in this book are examples only and are not intended to indicate 'correct' preferences in any way.)

3 Summary of Thinking Styles Criteria

'SENSORY' CRITERIA

Below is an example profile of someone's sensory scores. The scores indicate a kinaesthetic/visual preference, with a moderate auditory and digital score. Overall it is a profile which indicates a degree of flexibility across all the sensory thinking patterns.

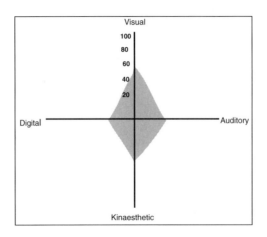

Visual processing involves the use of pictures and colour.
Auditory processing concerns the use of words and sounds.
Kinaesthetic processing involves feelings and emotions.
Digital processing is concerned with facts and data and may involve the use of abstract language.

Note: In this so-called Third Age or Information Age, it seemed appropriate to include digital thinking even though it is not an actual physical sense, although it often occurs in conjunction with other sensory processing.

'OTHER' CRITERIA

Below is an example of a profile for the Other Criteria. It indicates a degree of flexibility across all criteria, with a particular preference for options, internally referenced and differences. These three criteria have the highest percentage scores.

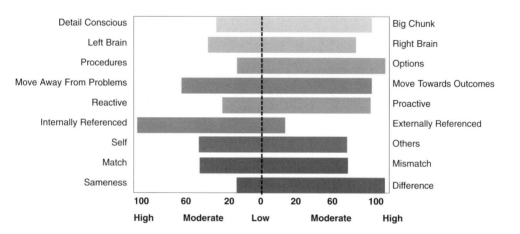

Detail Conscious thinking involves a preference for small, 'bite-sized' pieces of information.

Big Chunk thinking involves larger pieces of information, often in terms of key points or strategies.

Left Brain processing is logical and linear with information processed in sequence.

Right Brain thinking is creative, recognizes patterns and enables multi-tasking.

Procedures processing involves following instructions and the accepted way of doing things.

Options thinking involves a preference for choice and exploring what is possible.

People who process by *Moving Away From* problems avoid things which threaten their success.

People who process by *Moving Towards* outcomes are energized by accomplishment, by achieving their goals.

Reactive processing involves responding to situations or changes in circumstances.

Proactive processing means that people tend to initiate change and often plan for the future.

Internal processing involves checking within yourself, against your own judgements and standards.

External processing involves a reliance on feedback from sources outside yourself.

People who are *Self* referenced have themselves and their needs as their highest priority.

People who are *Others* referenced put the needs of other people first, over and above their own needs.

Processing by *Matching* involves agreement and a non-confrontational, collaborative approach.

Processing by *Mismatching* involves disagreement and often, challenging the status quo.

People who process via *Sameness* are motivated by stability; they will notice similarities.

People who process via *Differences* notice what is different; they have a high capacity for change.

'Sensory'
Thinking Styles

4 Visual

True wisdom consists not in seeing what is immediately before our eyes, but in foreseeing what is to come.
Terence, Roman dramatist

Visual processing can be either 'internal' or 'external' and is a preference for looking at information and seeing the issues.

'Visual internal' thinking involves creating pictures 'in your mind's eye', and often the use of visualization and imagery. As a relaxation technique, 'guided imagery' where as you listen to someone talking you imagine pictures in your mind, is easiest for those people who already have a preference for visual internal processing.

'Visual external' thinking involves the need to 'see' something physically. Someone with a preference for visual external processing will often draw a diagram or picture to explain to others what they mean or to think an issue through for themselves. They will also have a preference for any information which is presented in a visually interesting format, such as colourful graphs or landscapes.

Visual processing is very rapid, which means that sometimes visual thinkers can be impatient with others as they think more quickly. Visually oriented people are often quite upright in their posture and are likely to use their hands enthusiastically when speaking, most often at eye level or above to 'show' people what they mean.

PHILBERT WAS SHOWING EVERYONE HIS
VIEW OF THE COMPANY VISION

Visual thinkers often notice things other people miss and are great people 'watchers' who can't help but notice other people's behaviour and body language.

Language patterns for visual thinking can include: 'seeing what you mean', 'having a look', wanting to be 'clear', asking for 'clarification', or wanting to get some 'perspective' or 'focus' on an issue. Visual thinkers will be advocates for having a corporate 'vision'.

> *Where there is no vision, the people perish.*
> Bible, Old Testament (King James version)

Note: Do be aware that sometimes certain words are used as part of a corporate culture and become the accepted way of talking about issues rather than being representative of someone's actual thinking style.

Visually oriented people may dislike being stuck behind traffic when driving because their view is spoiled or because they cannot see where they are going clearly. They will prefer you to draw them a map rather than receiving long verbal directions, or they may make a visual map in their heads of whatever directions they receive verbally.

Excellent spellers use a visual strategy to remember words which they then look at and read off. Their visual strategy is quick, efficient and accurate. (You can buy a Spelling Strategy Pack from the charitable trust Thinking Styles in Education. Contact details are in Chapter 21.)

MANAGEMENT AND MOTIVATION
Motivate or manage visual thinkers by showing them what you will be looking for and what they can expect to see. Get them to buy into the corporate or departmental vision, and if you can, make sure that issues move forward quickly enough to maintain their interest.

As managers, visual thinkers will prefer proposals or reports to be short and to the point, preferably including the use of diagrams or models. If you give them a long wordy proposal they are unlikely to read it (although they may 'speed read' it), and will often only look at the executive summary in order to 'take a view'.

If companies really have a vision that is meaningful to
people and which they share, nothing will stop
them from being successful . . . A shared vision is
going to be a winning thing.
Warren G. Bennis

EXERCISES

To practise becoming more flexible on the visual scale:

◆ draw a picture and take a 'snap shot photograph' of it, then describe what it looks like in detail to someone else

◆ listen to some relaxing music and daydream, imagining a story or a film, adding colour if your first inclination is to use only black and white imagery

◆ watch the body language of one or two people in a meeting and observe how they interact

◆ play a game of Pictionary™ where you have to guess a word or object from a sketch or drawing

IN SUMMARY

✔	Visual
	➢ may visualize internally
	➢ use of visually presented information
	➢ very 'quick thinker'
	➢ may also speak very quickly
	➢ hand movements at eye level or above
	➢ can't help 'watching' people

WHAT'S YOUR SCORE?

Now that you have read this chapter you may want to estimate your degree of preference for this thinking style. Fill in your score below:

```
              0                                    100
   Visual     [                                        ]
            Low            Moderate            High
```

When you have estimated your score, transfer it to the Summary Profile in Chapter 17.

5 Auditory

There is one thing that matters –
to set a chime of words tinkling in the minds
of a few fastidious people.
Logan Pearsall Smith

Auditory thinking involves the use of words and sounds and the particular intonation of people's voices.

Someone with a preference for auditory thinking will communicate most easily through listening and talking to others or through reading and writing, and will sometimes prefer to use the telephone or write a memo rather than meet people in person.

MARK THOUGHT HE'D COME TO SEE GEARALD

As with all the sensory processing patterns, auditory thinking may be either internal or external. 'Auditory internal' processing happens when someone listens to their own internal dialogue in their heads, perhaps talking to themselves. 'Auditory external' involves actually physically talking an issue through, most often with someone else, although there are people who do 'talk out loud' to themselves.

Auditory thinking often involves being interested in words and their usage: linguistics such as skill with foreign languages, oratory, or a liking for reading, or an interest in poetry. Preferred pastimes may include reading books or playing word games such as crosswords, Scrabble or 'Call My Bluff'.

He [Winston Churchill] mobilized the English language and sent it into battle.
Ed Murrow

Auditory thinkers make very good listeners and often find it easy to repeat things back to you word-for-word. However, they may also paraphrase using their own favourite words, to which they can sometimes be very attached.

They are often easily distracted by background noise as they have a natural ability to 'overhear' other people's dialogue from across a room. They don't mean to 'eavesdrop' others' conversations deliberately, it's just something they cannot help doing!

Although for relaxation they frequently enjoy listening to music, in the workplace they often prefer to work in a quiet environment or even silence. Proposals or reports written by an auditory thinker can tend to be wordy and convoluted with pages and pages of plain text.

MANAGEMENT AND MOTIVATION

As managers, auditory thinkers are always willing to listen to an idea or hear someone out. They like written reports and proposals and will sometimes put instructions to their staff in writing.

To motivate auditory thinkers, be prepared to discuss issues with them and listen to their concerns and ideas. If they write to you, read what they have to say carefully and be prepared to comment on it so they know that you have taken the time to read it.

EXERCISES

To practise your auditory thinking:
- listen to the radio or a book on cassette
- listen to the 'silence' of the countryside identifying the sounds you hear
- tell a story using auditory props, e.g. *'the clip clopping sound of horses' hooves and the pitter patter of water droplets'*.
- talk an issue through with a colleague
- listen to music

IN SUMMARY

✔	Auditory
	➤ internal dialogue with self ➤ talk things through externally ➤ can't help 'overhearing' conversations ➤ music is very important ➤ likely to have 'language' skills ➤ use of specific words and tone important

WHAT'S YOUR SCORE?

Now that you have read this chapter you may want to estimate your degree of preference for this thinking style. Fill in your score below:

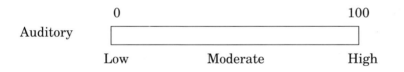

0		100
Auditory		
Low	Moderate	High

When you have estimated your score, transfer it to the Summary Profile in Chapter 17.

The voice so sweet, the words so fair,
As some soft chime had stroked the air;
And though the sound were parted thence,
Still left an echo in the sense.

Ben Jonson

6 Kinaesthetic

*People don't ask for facts in making up
their minds. They would rather have one good soul-
satisfying emotion than a dozen facts.*
Robert Keith Leavitt

Kinaesthetic thinking involves physical movement, feelings and emotions. Kinaesthetic thinkers process information through their bodies, both physically and emotionally.

'Kinaesthetic internal' thinking is emotional processing such as instincts or gut feelings which it is not possible to observe, although most people are able to identify other people's feelings such as joy, anger or pain from the look on their faces.

'Kinaesthetic external' thinking involves processing information via physical movement, for example walking or some other form of exercise, or foot and finger tapping; anything which we can see physically.

Kinaesthetic thinkers are the people who will tell you about how they 'feel' regarding an issue. People who process information in this way often speak slowly and deliberately and their language will contain phraseology which relates either to physical sensations, movement or their experience.

Kinaesthetic thinking is the sense most closely associated with emotional intelligence, which, thanks to Daniel Goleman, is now being recognized and valued in a business environment. Ten years ago when I was involved in management consultancy, 'touchy/feely' management skills were ridiculed and dismissed out of hand. I, for one, am very glad that this is now changing.

It is not that the Englishman can't feel – it is that he is afraid to feel. He has been taught at his public school that feeling is bad form.
E.M. Forster

Compared to a visually oriented person, kinaesthetically preferenced people think through and process information much more slowly, and they need to have the time to be able to do this, sometimes as much as two weeks, or even longer if they are emotionally attached to an issue.

Physical movement being very important, you will often see them walking about when they are thinking through a problem. If they cannot move and are forced to sit still (in a meeting for example or a classroom-style learning environment) it can adversely affect their thinking processes.

If you ask a kinaesthetically preferenced person a question, do not expect an immediate answer, as they will need more time than that, and remember that they will probably need to 'do' a task and experience it in order to learn it fully.

Kinaesthetic thinkers will often prefer to have a face-to-face meeting with others rather than use e-mail, the telephone or write a memo, as this provides an opportunity for personal contact. Socially, these people are often enthusiastic about physical interactions such as shaking hands or a touch on the arm. They are often described by the people who know them in terms such as 'genial', and 'amiable'.

MANAGEMENT AND MOTIVATION

As managers, kinaesthetic thinkers often care deeply for their staff and may take on a slightly 'parental' role, in that they feel responsible for the well-being of the people who work for them. They have a tendency to make decisions based on intuition or 'gut-feel', which can make it difficult for their staff to follow the logic of their decisions.

To manage or motivate kinaesthetic thinkers, give them the time they need to think through and process information, as it is this which enables them to function effectively. Talk with them face-to-face and be interested in how they feel about a project. If it's appropriate touch them; they will appreciate, for example, shaking hands or an arm around their shoulders to guide or support them.

EXERCISES

To practise your kinaesthetic processing:
- you may need to be more 'in touch' with your emotions, so think about how you feel about a variety of issues – some you care deeply about and others you are not so committed to
- explore your physical environment, perhaps by walking barefoot in the cool, wet grass of the morning dew, or by finding opportunities to experience physical sensations you are not so familiar with, such as the sharp taste of a lemon or the gnarled and knobbly feel of the bark of an old apple tree

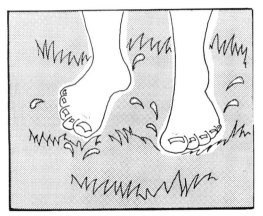

HARRY FELT CONVINCED THAT HIS DAILY
WATERING SESSION HELPED HIM STAY IN TOUCH
WITH HIS GRASS ROOTS ETHICS.

In Summary

✔	Kinaesthetic
	➣ emotional processing (gut feel, instinct comfort zone)
	➣ physical processing (movement)
	➣ thinking takes time
	➣ speech is slow and considered
	➣ enjoy sensory experience (touch/feel)
	➣ emotionally committed to work or colleagues

HI HARRY, STILL GETTING TO GRIPS WITH THE
TOUCHY FEELY STUFF, I SEE

WHAT'S YOUR SCORE?

Now that you have read this chapter you may want to estimate your degree of preference for this thinking style. Fill in your score below:

	0	100
Kinaesthetic		
	Low	Moderate	High

When you have estimated your score, transfer it to the Summary Profile in Chapter 17.

Rem tene; verba sequentur
Grasp the subject; the words will follow.
Cato, the Elder

7 Digital

Let's call a bed a bed – not a 'device or arrangement that may be used to let patients lie down when the need to do so is a consequence of the patient's condition, rather than a need for active intervention', as it was famously described.

Frank Dobson

Digital thinking is concerned with facts and data and may involve the use of abstract language. Digital thinkers use language which lacks any sensory reference. Their style of processing is linear and logical which means that they frequently use long complicated sentences, often including the use of their industry jargon.

Digital processing is not a physical 'sense', but rather a focus on facts and the discrete content of communication. I have included it here with the Sensory Criteria as 'digital thinking' often occurs in conjunction with other sensory processing. For example, many of us will have met the rather 'bumbling' university professor with their somewhat untidy appearance, 'cuddly tummy', beard and cardigan (kinaesthetic digital); or at the other extreme, the good looking technical expert with their smart shiny shoes and striking appearance who inundates you with information and figures (visual digital).

Digital processors are highly data rational and are happy to become involved in the analysis of tables and statistics, particularly as they have a tendency to dislike ambiguity which is one of the reasons why digital thinkers make good scientists and academics. At the extreme these people can be loners who do not make good team players and who can sometimes lack social, inter-personal skills.

Highly intelligent, many digitally referenced people are to be found in the corridors of academic institutions, research environments or the legal professions, where they have the opportunity to work more independently.

Interestingly, many digital thinkers, if they have *only* a digital preference, are not concerned with other sensory stimuli, such as the way their environment looks or feels, the clothes they wear or the food they eat. I have one particular friend, a highly digital thinker, who told me, 'I eat only to refuel or I would cease to function effectively.' He reminds me of Data the android in *Star Trek*.

Some people actively use a digital processing pattern to avoid (or keep in check) their feelings about certain issues or when they find themselves in a certain set of circumstances. It is quite common for some people to use this preference as a kind of 'protective barrier' within which they encase themselves when they are under pressure or have been panicked in some way.

'Going Digital' is a very good way of avoiding an emotional response. I have been told by a number of medical doctors that, so as not to become emotionally involved with the conditions of their patients, they need to keep themselves 'disassociated', i.e. uninvolved, in order to be able to respond quickly and appropriately, particularly in a crisis.

MANAGEMENT AND MOTIVATION
Because they can sometimes be described as loners who avoid interactions with others, highly digital thinkers tend not to make very good managers, as they can lack the inter-personal skills necessary for the role.

To manage such people, give them comprehensive instructions and a full workload, respecting their need for complexity.

EXERCISES
To practise developing your digital skills:
◆ read a technical textbook or an academic article
◆ write a legal letter, or a letter to a solicitor in the third person detailing the circumstances surrounding an imaginary incident
◆ write long complex sentences using the jargon of your industry

We must further individualize our training efforts,
because the job needs of our people will become more
unique, and we will find a rising proportion of training
assignments involving a single individual,
or at most a very limited number.
Jerome P. Lysaught

✔	Digital
	➤ like complexity
	➤ focus on the facts
	➤ may lack interpersonal skills
	➤ recognized as 'intelligent'
	➤ often prefer detail
	➤ disinterested in food, clothes, surroundings

WHAT'S YOUR SCORE?

Now that you have read this chapter you may want to estimate your degree of preference for this thinking style. Fill in your score below:

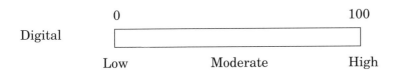

When you have estimated your score, transfer it to the Summary Profile in Chapter 17.

The real danger is not that computers will begin to think like men, but that men will begin to think like computers.
Sydney Harris

You will now have completed your Sensory Thinking Styles Profile. Your scores for the four sensory criteria are 'absolute' scores out of a possible 100. If you have transferred the scores onto the blank grid in Chapter 17, some of you will have a diamond shape, others a triangle and perhaps others a straight line or even a solitary cross or dot. Also, your shape may be larger or smaller than other people's. These reflect your uniqueness and individuality regarding your thinking processes and preferences.

I have seen 'diamonds' of all imaginable sizes and shapes, so whatever the shape of your particular diamond, it will be 'right for you'. You probably know yourself better than anyone, so trust yourself that your scores are an accurate reflection of your thinking styles. Remember that the score you give yourself should reflect your *degree of preference* for that style and is *not* an indication of your ability.

For many of you your scores and shape will not be a surprise. For others, what might come as a surprise is that anyone else could possibly think in a different way from you!

I have said the following things elsewhere in the book, however they are worth repeating: First, there are no right or wrong answers, only personal preferences regarding processing styles. Second, I strongly believe that, in the next century, it will be people's flexibility and in particular their cognitive flexibility regarding their thinking styles, that will lead to individual and organizational success.

'Other'
Thinking Styles

Detail Conscious and Big Chunk Strategic

It is impossible for all things to be precisely set down in writing; for rules must be universal, but actions are concerned with particulars.

Aristotle

This thinking style relates to the size of information a person has a natural preference for and will be comfortable with. The bigger the preference for the 'chunk size', the less information will be required.

LEARNING AND CHUNK SIZE

Anyone can learn anything if it's presented to them in the appropriate chunk size for <u>them</u>.

Julia Miller, editor

The more we think about this statement and about the chunk size we ourselves prefer to receive information in when we learn most effectively, the more sense it begins to make. I wish I had known this when I started my career as a management trainer ten years ago! There are still many trainers and, dare I say it, teachers, who teach or train others in the way which suits *themselves* best rather than the learner.

Note: Be aware though that even the most detail conscious learner will usually need to have an 'overview' first so they know exactly where to insert the details.

You've got to think about 'big things' while you're doing the small things so that all the small things go in the right direction.

Alvin Toffler

DETAIL CONSCIOUS THINKING

Those people with a preference for detailed thinking are both meticulous and tenacious and tend to have high standards, taking their time to work through tasks. They are usually very thorough and will finish a job once they have started it, if at all possible. They like to receive detailed information and they also disseminate information in small chunks, which can be quite time-consuming and frustrating to anyone with a larger chunk size than theirs!

HI JOHN, STILL UP TO YOUR EYES IN DETAIL,
I SEE

Behaviourally, someone with a preference for details often finds it easy to concentrate, although they can sometimes have a tendency towards perfectionism and may be described as intense people. They tend not to like being disturbed when they are working and do not welcome interruptions as they are very focused on their tasks.

Detail conscious thinkers will usually think of time in terms of days, weeks and possibly months rather than years (which often precludes them from strategic planning), and they are ideally suited to job roles where attention to detail, organization, repetitive tasks and analysis are important. This might sound rather obvious, but I often come across people in organizations with a big chunk preference who are being asked to complete detailed tasks. Not surprisingly, they make mistakes which they find frustrating and which can sometimes adversely affect their careers as they become labelled as 'sloppy' workers where details are concerned.

MANAGEMENT AND MOTIVATION
To manage detail conscious thinkers you will need to give them clear and detailed instructions as they dislike ambiguity. Give them enough time to do what they would consider to be a 'proper job'. Provide them with a structure for reviewing progress regularly and let them know that you are available for them should they require any further details.

As managers, people with a preference for detail can sometimes hold the reins rather too tightly for their staff, and their desire for detail can sometimes be perceived as being fastidious and over-demanding, perhaps even unnecessary. They need to ensure that they are available to their staff and do not become overly focused on their own tasks.

EXERCISES
To practise developing your detailed thinking:
- proofread a memo, proposal or report, adding detail and checking spelling
- complete your tax return, reading all the explanatory notes and filling in all the boxes
- write a detailed inventory of one room in your house (as you would do for an insurance claim)

BIG CHUNK THINKING
Those with a preference for big chunk thinking want the overview or a general impression of a topic. They are not interested in the details and can become quite impatient with anyone who tries to give them too much information. They may pay attention to details the first time they come across them, but then largely gloss over them in the future. This means that they are not good at administrative or maintenance activities which require thoroughness and which they may have to repeat periodically.

> *You cannot argue with someone who*
> *denies the first principles.*
> Aristotle

Senior management is responsible for defining corporate strategy and big chunk thinkers make excellent strategists. In fact, an ability to think in this way: 'the big picture, overview' or 'think in the longer term' is a pre-requisite for a senior management position. I have noticed in business that a strategy meeting, i.e. a meeting to decide what to do rather than how to do it, will take twice or even three times as long as it should if it is attended by anyone other than big chunk thinkers.

To conquer the enemy without resorting to war is the most desirable. The highest form of generalship is to conquer the enemy by strategy.
Sun Tzu

MANAGEMENT AND MOTIVATION
As managers big chunk thinkers are good at providing direction and will often be flexible regarding how their staff achieve the objectives they have been set. They may need to be reminded of important details, however, because potentially these can be overlooked. This means that in order to be truly effective, big chunk thinkers really need efficient teams with the flexibility for details to support them.

When managing those with a preference for strategic thinking, play to their strengths and don't bog them down with details or repetitive tasks as they are likely to make mistakes. Motivate them by giving them 'key points' and letting them know how their input relates to departmental or corporate strategy.

EXERCISES
To practise developing your big chunk thinking:
♦ jot down only the key points of a report or a proposal
♦ identify some targets or ultimate goal (leaving the details of how you will achieve them until another time)
♦ consider or review your 'lifetime strategy' – those things that you would like to achieve in your lifetime, planning in terms of years

✔	Detail Conscious
	➤ small pieces of information
	➤ conscientious with details
	➤ interested in details
	➤ take time to process as dealing with more information

✔	Big Chunk Strategic
	➤ prefer general principles
	➤ make mistakes with details
	➤ not interested in details
	➤ focus on key points
	➤ process quickly

WHAT'S YOUR SCORE?

Now that you have read this chapter you may want to estimate your degree of preference for these thinking styles. Fill in your score below:

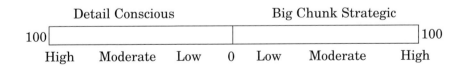

	Detail Conscious				Big Chunk Strategic		
100							100
	High	Moderate	Low	0	Low	Moderate	High

When you have estimated your scores, transfer them to the Summary Profile in Chapter 17.

9 Left and Right Brain

Some people are aware of another sort of thinking which . . . leads to those simple ideas that are obvious only after they have been thought of . . . the term 'lateral thinking' has been coined to describe this other sort of thinking, 'vertical thinking' is used to denote the conventional logical process.

Edward de Bono

These thinking styles relate to which of the brain's hemispheres you naturally access when thinking. Are you creative and spontaneous in your thinking or do you think things through systematically and logically?

LEFT BRAIN THINKING

People with a left brain dominance have a preference for order and logical sequence. They are easy to identify because they will always start at the beginning and work systematically through a task to the end. Wherever possible they will finish what they have started. If you interrupt them halfway through, they will probably start again – from the beginning! This can be very frustrating for their opposites – those with a right brain dominance, but is, of course, completely logical to them!

Not easily distracted, left brain thinkers are usually highly organized, focused and thorough individuals who find it easy to concentrate on the task in hand. They like writing lists and are very good at time management, always arriving on time for meetings and appointments. In fact, they usually hate tardiness, untidiness or sloppiness in any form and this is most evident when you examine their working space, which is invariably neat and tidy. They set themselves their own deadlines, starting at the beginning and allowing themselves time to finish often well before the due date. These traits are in stark contrast to someone with a right brain preference, whose working space can best be described as 'creative', but will appear 'chaotic and untidy' to the untrained eye.

PHILBERT BEGAN TO THINK THAT SHARING AN OFFICE WITH JOE FROM MARKETING WASN'T SUCH A GOOD IDEA AFTER ALL

Left brain thinkers do not multi-task, they like to do one thing at a time and do it properly. If you give them too many tasks, or try to hurry them, they will become flustered and possibly stressed. They excel in any job role which requires a logical and tenacious approach, especially where they also have the opportunity to 'tie up loose ends' and ensure that the job is properly finished and completed to their satisfaction.

MANAGEMENT AND MOTIVATION

As managers, left brain thinkers are focused and logical, like things to be done thoroughly and will expect reports or proposals to be sequential and ordered.

To manage these people give them clear instructions as they dislike ambiguity, and ideally, give them job roles where they can complete tasks, especially as they often enjoy administrative and maintenance activities.

EXERCISES

To practise developing your left brain, logical thinking skills:
- fill in a form starting at the beginning and systematically working through to the end
- write a list of things you need to do
- use the phone listening with your right ear as this connects directly with your left brain hemisphere

RIGHT BRAIN THINKING

Right brain thinkers have a natural ability to multi-task, and are often found doing half a dozen things at the same time. These people think and work very quickly, however, they can be easily distracted and may have a tendency to cut corners.

They are frequently highly creative and artistic, excelling in job roles which include an element of design or where they can give their imagination a free rein. They sometimes dislike rules and boundaries, feeling that this limits their creativity. They do not function well in environments they perceive as 'over-controlling', in which case they cease to function.

One of the advantages of being disorderly is that one is constantly making exciting discoveries.
A.A. Milne

Time management is not easy for right brain thinkers and they prefer to be given deadlines. Even then they have a tendency to leave everything until the last minute and stay up late or get up early in order to finish on time. They are invariably late as they will try to fit too many things into too short a time-frame. To be on time they tend to have to over-compensate and so will actually arrive early.

I've been on a calendar, but never on time.
Marilyn Monroe

You may have noticed for yourself that 'creative thinkers think backwards'. By this I mean that if you ask them a question, they will very quickly 'go to the end' and know the answer. If you ask them to explain how they worked that answer out, they will have to 'think backwards' to the starting point of their thinking and then run their calculation more logically forwards. This more logical 'left brained' approach of 'thinking forwards from beginning to end', takes them much longer to do, in contrast with their natural right brain thinking which is very quick indeed.

Creative thinkers are not great list people, preferring to carry information around in their heads rather than write it down. This is a mistake, as their brains cannot distinguish between what they have done (and can mentally tick off) and what they have only thought about doing. Consequently they often forget tasks and may need to be reminded by colleagues.

MANAGEMENT AND MOTIVATION

To manage right brain thinkers, motivate them by giving them variety in their jobs and allowing them to be creative in their own way. Assign them target dates and deadlines to work to, allowing them some flexibility regarding when they do a task, remembering to check progress from time to time.

As managers they tend to be high-energy individuals who can successfully manage a large number of people and projects at the same time. However, they can lose focus as they switch between projects and may need to be reminded of the organization's immediate priorities.

EXERCISES

To practise developing your right brain thinking skills:
◆ draw a picture using colour in some way
◆ spend some time daydreaming
◆ give your imagination a free rein to redesign your garden or a room in your house
◆ brainstorm ideas for a party
◆ tell a story, making it up as you go

WHOLE BRAIN THINKING

It is worth writing a short note on 'whole brain thinking'. This is when you access both left and right brain hemispheres together and is one of the key principles of accelerated learning techniques.

To connect both brain hemispheres for whole brain thinking, listen to music, ideally, the kind of music which mimics the brain's alpha state brainwave patterns such as baroque music and most of Mozart's work. This is why Don

Campbell developed the term 'the Mozart effect' to describe increased performance by school children after listening to Mozart's music.

Another exercise is to put your hands together and press your fingertips and thumbs together applying gentle rhythmic pressure, opening your hands if that is more comfortable. This brain gym exercise crosses the body's natural 'meridian line' which runs vertically down the centre of the body and hence links both brain hemispheres.

Research has shown that whole brain thinking is more effective than accessing either of the two brain hemispheres independently. If we think about some of the people throughout history whom we would consider to be geniuses such as Leonardo da Vinci or Einstein, it becomes obvious that they displayed both 'left brain logical' and 'right brain creative' talents simultaneously.

For more information on whole brain thinking, Accelerated Learning and brain gym refer to Chapters 20 and 22.

Discovery consists of seeing what everybody has seen and thinking what nobody has thought.
Albert von Szent-Gyorgyi

In Summary

✔	Left Brain
	➤ logical
	➤ sequential, linear processing
	➤ think 'forwards' from the question to the answer
	➤ tend not to think 'out of the box'
	➤ complete one task then move on to the next
	➤ focused, compelled to complete a task where possible

✔	Right Brain
	➤ creative
	➤ 'chaotic' thinking
	➤ think 'backwards' from the answer, back to the question
	➤ recognize patterns and make connections
	➤ multi-tasking
	➤ easily distracted and not compelled to finish a task

What's Your Score?

Now that you have read this chapter you may want to estimate your degree of preference for these thinking styles. Fill in your score below:

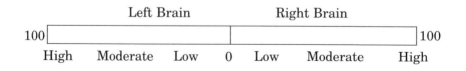

	Left Brain				Right Brain		
100							100
	High	Moderate	Low	0	Low	Moderate	High

When you have estimated your scores, transfer them to the Summary Profile in Chapter 17.

MEN AND WOMEN

Early figures from our research indicate that in the UK in a work context, approximately 70% of men have a left brain preference for linear and logical thinking, and approximately 70% of women a right brain preference. In other words, only 30% of men find it easy to multi-task and only 30% of women are perceived as logical.

10 Procedures and Options

*Even if I had to follow a procedure, I'd have to
have flexibility and choice in how I did it.
Otherwise I'd go nuts!*

Tina Bettison, the Maverick Team

These thinking styles relate to whether a person is motivated by deciding on their own course of action or whether they prefer to follow an established method of doing things.

PROCEDURAL THINKING

People with a procedural preference like to do things the 'right' way and they will not deviate from the accepted process. Once they have started a task they are compelled to finish it. They tend not to like too much variety in their job and are happy to repeat tasks or processes again and again preferring to follow a formula which is already set down and defined rather than designing their own way of doing things.

Procedural thinkers wouldn't dream of trying to alter or improve a process, and can be rather 'rule bound' as a result. Disliking taking the initiative, they do well in job roles where adherence to procedures is important or in any administrative post. These people are, of course, quite capable of making choices and taking decisions. However, within the workplace they tend to prefer to operate within predefined boundaries, and may not be prepared to make a decision. Rather, they will present you with the facts and accepted procedures of a case, leaving it up to management to make the choice. They will willingly follow the instructions of those they consider qualified to give them.

MANAGEMENT AND MOTIVATION

As managers, procedural thinkers will always be scrupulously fair, although they can be perceived as inflexible at times. They are concerned that their staff do things the 'right' way, ensuring that relevant protocols are followed.

When managing someone with a procedural preference, motivate them by teaching them the 'correct' way to do something, appreciate them for their tenacity and give them time to complete the processes for whatever tasks you give them.

EXERCISES
To practise becoming more procedurally flexible:
◆ follow a list of instructions exactly and complete a task from start to finish
◆ complete your own tax return form, reading all of the explanatory notes before you start
◆ follow a meal by meal 'healthy eating food plan' or diet for three days

OPTIONS THINKING

Opportunities and possibilities motivate options thinkers. They believe that there is always an alternative, and moreover, that they have a choice about which alternative to use. They like to do things the 'most appropriate' way, i.e. they believe that there is more than one way of doing something.

PHILBERT MISTAKENLY THOUGHT THAT BEING
GIVEN A PARKING TICKET HAD BEEN A MATTER
OF CHOICE

When stuck 'between a rock and a hard place' you may
hear these people say that they 'have no choice', or 'it's the
only option'. This is still options language. They believe
that they can always improve on an idea or a process. This
means, therefore, that they are happy to review and revise
a proposal if asked.   Interestingly, writing a procedure is
an options activity and following it a procedural activity!

Those with a preference for options thinking love to start
new projects although they are not compelled to finish
them. They like a challenge and are highly motivated

problem-solvers enjoying thinking up ways of overcoming obstacles. Sometimes they can have difficulty committing to a task or course of action if they think that it will 'limit their options' at a later date. These people use the language of possibility, i.e. they will respond well to a suggestion that they 'could' do something, but not that they 'should' do something. Options thinkers enjoy making decisions although they can sometimes have difficulty if they are 'spoilt for choice' and have too many options, each of which is attractive in some way. They thrive on variety and their ideal job is one where they have a degree of autonomy and responsibility for decision-making.

MANAGEMENT AND MOTIVATION

To manage options thinkers focus on the outcome and give them some flexibility in how they achieve their targets. Motivate them by allowing them to prioritize their workload. Wherever possible, let them have input into decisions regarding which projects or tasks they will be involved with. They may dislike being told what to do and especially how to do it because that reduces their options, so ideally give them variety in their work and a degree of autonomy.

As managers, options thinkers can be good decision-makers, although they can sometimes change their minds rather too frequently for those who work below them, so they must pay attention to ensuring that they are always consistent or they can confuse their staff. Generally optimistic in nature, they believe that there is always a solution and they will usually be happy to bend the rules in order to find a flexible outcome which supports their staff.   They are keen on opportunities which would allow them or their people to learn something new or develop existing skills.

To practise developing your options thinking:

◆ think about the ways in which you could spend your time at the weekend

◆ go to a restaurant and spend some time perusing the menu and thinking of the combinations of food you could have, then really enjoy making your choice

◆ think about a decision which you will be making in the near future and consider the implications of each of the choices you could make

Note: It is worth mentioning here that decision-making is all about making choices and every decision is, by definition, limiting in some way.

When you have to make a choice and don't make it,
that is in itself a choice.
William James

IN SUMMARY

✔	Procedures
	➤ believe there is a 'right' way
	➤ like following procedures
	➤ motivated by correctness
	➤ compelled to complete a procedure once started
	➤ prefer others to decide
	➤ don't need choice

✔	Options
	➢ believe in alternatives
	➢ like writing procedures
	➢ motivated by possibility
	➢ change track easily and will take short-cuts if possible
	➢ like decision-making
	➢ dislike choices being limited

WHAT'S YOUR SCORE?

Now that you have read this chapter you may want to estimate your degree of preference for these thinking styles. Fill in your score below:

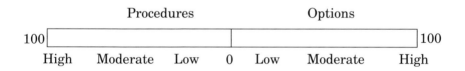

	Procedures				Options		
100							100
	High	Moderate	Low	0	Low	Moderate	High

When you have estimated your scores, transfer them to the Summary Profile in Chapter 17.

Systems represent someone's attempt at a solution to problems, but they do not solve problems, they produce complicated responses.
Melvin Sykes

We can believe what we choose. We are answerable for what we choose to believe.
John Henry Newman

11 Move Away From Problems and Move Towards Outcomes

When the wind blows some people build walls,
others build windmills.

Peter Hawkins

These thinking styles relate to the direction in which a person moves, in order to motivate themselves regarding their goals. They will either move towards the attainment of their objectives, or they will move away from something which would prevent them from getting what they want.

MOVING AWAY FROM PROBLEMS THINKING

People with a preference for moving away from problems are energized by threats to their success. They will tell you what they *don't* want rather than what they do want, which can lead to them being perceived as negative, jaded or cynical, especially by those who have a preference for moving towards outcomes. It is important to understand that they are not being negative, it's just the way that their brain works. Their brain processes in such a way as to make them appear negative.

These people can easily identify what is wrong – shortfalls, weaknesses, potential problems or impending disaster. This makes them excellent trouble-shooters, although at the extreme, they can be easily distracted by the latest problem and can have a tendency to fall into crisis management, sometimes even creating a crisis for them to then solve.

Move away from problems thinkers are very concerned with avoiding making a mistake and this can sometimes lead to inaction. They make good proofreaders as they notice inaccuracies and what is wrong. They would rather mend something now than have to fix it later, believing that 'a stitch in time saves nine'. This makes them keen on preventative maintenance activities and very good at contingency planning. Because it is the thought of an absolute cut-off point which motivates them, they will also tend to talk about deadlines rather than goals, targets or key dates.

CHRIS ALWAYS MADE SURE HE HAD AT LEAST
TWO OF EVERYTHING JUST IN CASE
SOMETHING WENT WRONG

MANAGEMENT AND MOTIVATION

As managers, people who have a preference for moving away from problems thinking can be cautious, as they like to be sure that their staff have planned adequately for contingencies in order to avoid potential costly mistakes. This means that they can be difficult to please where proposals and reports are concerned and may be overzealous in their focus on potential mistakes, possible problems or anything which could be 'difficult' or might 'get worse'. At the other extreme they can be caught up in crisis management and continually driven by the short-term priorities of problem-solving which can mean that they 'forget' the tasks they gave their staff the previous week or month.

To manage those with an away from problems thinking pattern, give them deadlines to work to. While you can make them aware of what the objectives are, focus their attention on what you want to avoid and what the potential problems might be. Value their ability for contingency planning and be aware of their propensity for fire-fighting, as they can sometimes find it such a motivator that they create problems just so that they can 'solve' them!

SALES AND MARKETING

It is interesting how sales and marketing departments have recognized the importance of these particular criteria. Notice how pensions and investment companies suggest to people that they should 'save to create a better future' for themselves (a towards orientation), in order to 'avoid falling into the poverty trap' in their old age (away from). Life insurance companies persuade their customers to buy life insurance to 'guard against' their families being left in financial 'difficulties' should they die (away from), and to give them 'security and peace of mind' (towards), and again, to 'create a more secure future for your family' (towards).

PROJECT MANAGEMENT

Project managers require a unique combination of skills and a high degree of flexibility regarding both thinking and management style, not only for the two criteria examined in this chapter but for all the thinking styles. For example, on a project team a balance of people will help to ensure that goals and targets are set (towards), contingency plans are made (away from), a focus is maintained on priorities (towards), and problems are solved (away from).

Note: It is a personal theory of mine that in the twenty-first century the focus of management and teamwork will shift from the current hierarchical pyramid with the manager at the top, to a 'project based' approach where the following occur:

- teams are cross-functional and inter-departmental
- the manager works for the team rather than the team working for and being 'managed' by the manager
- someone may be a member of more than one project team at a time
- project teams are trans-national, linked by internet technology and intranets
- project teams include members from outside an organization, e.g. its customer, competitor and supplier networks
- members of project teams are freelance and not solely employed by one organization, brought in for their specialist skills and expertise

A few of you reading this may already be working in some of the ways outlined. For example: journalism, the music industry, theatre and films all have elements of 'project-based teamwork' involved in current working practices. For others of you, what I have written will seem light years away.

MOVING TOWARDS OUTCOMES
People who have a preference for moving towards outcomes are motivated by accomplishment, by what they can 'get, gain, have or achieve'. They like to be involved in the creation or achievement of a goal, such as a corporate vision, for example. If they do recognize potential problems, they tend to play them down, gloss over or ignore them, saying that 'we'll cross that bridge when we come to it', which can lead to people thinking them naive, especially those who move away from problems. They are not easily distracted, finding it easy to stay focused on the outcome and they are good at managing priorities. They are ideally suited to job roles where the focus is on achieving a defined objective or where they are responsible for the creation of something. Very often these people move towards change of some kind or towards the future.

MANAGEMENT AND MOTIVATION
To manage towards outcomes thinkers, focus on the goal, give them their own targets and tell them what needs to be accomplished. Involve them, explaining what the benefits will be to them and what they will get as a result of achieving their objectives.

As managers, towards outcomes thinkers are interested in the advantages of a particular course of action – ways for them and their team to learn, develop or gain experience, and anything that will help them achieve their department's goals.

EXERCISES
To practise developing your towards outcomes thinking:
◆ focus on an outcome or a dream you want to attain
◆ set some achievable targets for the above
◆ think of the kind of future that you would want to create for yourself and focus on the ways that you can bring those elements into your life now

IN SUMMARY

✔	Move Away From Problems
	➢ say what they don't want
	➢ make contingency plans
	➢ motivated by threats
	➢ believe things will get worse
	➢ use 'negative' language
	➢ 'stick' people

✔	Move Towards Outcomes
	➢ tell you what they want
	➢ set goals and targets
	➢ motivated by success
	➢ ignore/play down problems
	➢ use 'positive' language
	➢ 'carrot' people

WHAT'S YOUR SCORE?

Now that you have read this chapter you may want to estimate your degree of preference for these thinking styles. Fill in your score below:

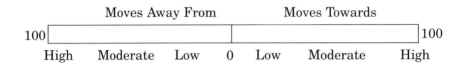

When you have estimated your scores, transfer them to the Summary Profile in Chapter 17.

Three people were at work on a construction site. All three were doing the same job, but when each was asked what his job was, the answers varied. 'Breaking rocks,' the first replied. 'Earning my living,' the second said. 'Helping to build a cathedral,' said the third.
Peter Schultz

Obstacles are things a person sees when he takes his eyes off his goal.
E. Joseph Cossman

12 Reactive and Proactive

There are really only three types of people: those who
make things happen, those who watch things happen,
and those who say, 'What happened?'
Ann Landers

These thinking styles relate to how you motivate
yourself to take some course of action. Do you take
the initiative yourself, or do you wait for someone or
something else to happen before you act?

REACTIVE THINKING
People with a preference for reactive thinking respond to
others or to the situation. They like to understand their
environment fully, so they often require clarification or
more information. (They don't want to control their
environment, just understand it.) Reactive thinkers are
best suited to a role where they need to respond to requests
from others or where it's important to study situations and
circumstances before committing to a course of action.

These people are often thoughtful and cautious in nature.
They are also frequently preoccupied with the
consequences of their actions and because they want to be
certain that they have made the right decision, sometimes
they think that it is best to do nothing rather than make
the wrong decision.

Reactive thinkers tend to wait, and will either delay, waiting for the situation to be absolutely right before acting, or they will wait for someone else to initiate some action before joining in. Where time is of the essence, for example if a deal is to be made or a purchase agreed, they can sometimes require so much information that any advantage is lost.

Forty thousand wishes won't fill your bucket with fishes.
Fisherman's saying

MANAGEMENT AND MOTIVATION

When managing someone with a preference for reactive thinking, help them to understand fully the implications of their role or the projects they are involved with. Work to their strengths allowing them time to analyse and plan rather than pushing them to start immediately. Give them time to think things through and invite them to respond.

As managers they may need to be encouraged to agree on and commit to a course of action. Remember that they will react badly to those who work for them trying to push them into a decision before they are ready. To get their support show that you have considered every eventuality and have been thorough in your planning.

EXERCISES
To practise your reactive thinking skills:
◆ spend time analysing a given situation before acting
◆ wait, rather than responding to a situation immediately
◆ instead of picking up the phone, draft a letter or memo, then wait a day or two before sending it
◆ if you have a problem to resolve as a result of something that has happened, sleep on it and return to it the next day

PROACTIVE THINKING

People with a preference for proactive thinking are the initiators, they love to start new projects. They really get things done and will be the people who organize action groups, sit on committees and plan social events. Very excited by new ideas and the latest project, they are not compelled to finish what they have started and may move on to the next thing before any real progress has been made. They frequently embrace change and like to be among the innovators who make change happen.

MUST DO SOMETHING ABOUT THE LIGHTING IN
HERE CAN HARDLY SEE A THING

HA! MUCH BETTER! NOTHING LIKE BEING PROACTIVE

I see myself as a doer. I'm sure that other people have had ideas that were similar to mine. The difference is that I have carried mine into action and they have not.
Nolan Bushnell

Proactive thinkers often want to start their pet projects immediately and although they may like to plan things out, they can have a tendency to act with little or no forethought or consideration for the consequences of their actions. This means that sometimes they can fail to think things through and they have a tendency to implement the first solution they think of, discovering later that by talking to a few more people or gathering just a little more information they would have reached a different conclusion.

At best, proactive thinkers can be focused and highly motivated achievers. At worst, they can be very controlling, bulldozing others in their rush to implement their ideas in their way.

I am certainly not one of those who needs to be prodded. In fact, if anything, I am a prod.
Sir Winston Churchill

MANAGEMENT AND MOTIVATION
As managers, proactive thinkers are high-energy individuals who are full of ideas, and are enthusiastic and supportive of their staff. Their greatest weakness is that they can sometimes shift the goalposts and pursue their latest project while leaving their staff to pick up the pieces behind them. This tends to happen particularly if they have encouraged their subordinates to jump in without undertaking the necessary analysis first.

To manage proactive thinkers successfully, be mindful that they can easily become frustrated and bored, so motivate them by giving them variety in their work, and allow them to be involved in projects where they can 'get on with things and get things done'. They may need to be managed actively in order to focus their energies and they do need to feel that in some way their involvement has contributed to moving an issue or project forward.

EXERCISE
To develop your proactive thinking skills:
♦ begin a project that you have been considering
♦ limit the amount of analysis you carry out before taking a decision
♦ rather than putting off taking action, do it!
♦ go shopping and buy the first thing that you really like and can afford

IN SUMMARY

✔	Reactive
	➢ wait for information
	➢ respond to circumstances
	➢ 'cautious' in nature
	➢ consider results/effects of their actions
	➢ will analyse and plan

✔	Proactive
	➤ take or initiate action ➤ impatient if made to wait ➤ may be impetuous or impulsive ➤ don't consider consequences of their actions ➤ prefer to jump straight in

WHAT'S YOUR SCORE?

Now that you have read this chapter you may want to estimate your degree of preference for these thinking styles. Fill in your score below:

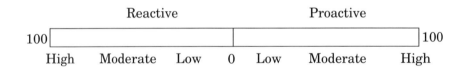

Reactive	Proactive

100 | | 100
High   Moderate   Low   0   Low   Moderate   High

When you have estimated your scores, transfer them to the Summary Profile in Chapter 17.

13 Internally and Externally Referenced

Self confidence is important.
Confidence in others is essential.
William A. Schreyer

These thinking styles relate to how people 'know' they have done a good job or are doing the right thing. Do they have their own internal standards and criteria by which to judge, i.e. they find the answers 'internally' within themselves, or do they rely on 'external' sources, such as feedback from other people?

THE TRAINER THOUGHT IT WOULD BE A GOOD IDEA
TO SPLIT THE GROUP

Internally Referenced Thinking

People with a preference for internally referenced thinking maintain and evaluate their standards within themselves. They instinctively 'know' whether something is right or not. They are very good at decision-making (even if they sometimes make the 'wrong' decisions!) because they are very self-confident and can be quite forceful in their beliefs. There is a note of caution here, however, because an extremely high score on this scale means that a person could be described as over-confident, arrogant or self-opinionated, as they may well ignore the advice and opinions of others.

> *Self trust is the first secret of success.*
> Ralph Waldo Emerson

Quick to judge, they tend to dislike being judged by other people, particularly if that judgement does not match their own. Their positive traits are that they are often dynamic, strong-willed and independent, and are likely to possess many 'leadership' qualities.

Interestingly, the amount of feedback received from others is often very important. Sometimes one or two pieces of adverse feedback may be dismissed, but when the third or fourth piece is received, that is the point at which an internally referenced thinker begins to listen. At the extreme, of course, someone with a very high score on this scale will dismiss all criticism as either unimportant, invalid, or not relevant, still insisting that they are right to the very end.

I don't mind how much my ministers talk, as long as they do what I say.
Margaret Thatcher

MANAGEMENT AND MOTIVATION

Internally referenced thinkers can be easy to manage because they are confident, quite like to work independently on projects and need little direction from their managers. They will work well in a team provided there are few internal disagreements and they believe in what they are doing. If, however, they do not respect their managers, or they disagree with the decisions that have been made, it can become very difficult to focus them on their tasks and ensure that they do as they have been asked.

As managers they tend to be good decision-makers who are supportive of their staff. Potentially, though, highly internally referenced managers may not pay enough attention to the feedback they receive from the people who work with or for them. This can lead to frustration if their staff or colleagues don't feel they are being listened to.

EXERCISES

To practise becoming more internally referenced:
- develop your own set of standards for some tasks so that you can evaluate your own performance
- make a decision regarding something you are strongly committed to and support it, even against dissenting feedback from others
- judge for yourself how well you have done on a particular project or task

It is worth mentioning here that many people's thinking pattern could best be described as 'internally referenced with an external check'. This means that these people are pretty sure they are doing and thinking the right thing, however they do like to check with a few select friends or colleagues whose opinions they respect. They will then 'go back within themselves' to double-check internally again, as shown in diagram A below.

Some people will always double-check with someone else, others only check when they are not completely certain that they are right, and others when they have received some adverse feedback.

DIAGRAM A

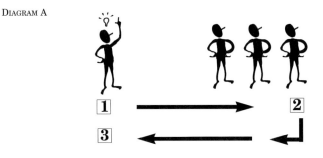

There are other people whose processing pattern could be best described as 'externally referenced with an internal check'. With this processing pattern, someone will talk with others to gain initial feedback and then check this information against their own criteria and standards, and then return to double-check with others once again that they are indeed on the right track, as shown in diagram B.

DIAGRAM B

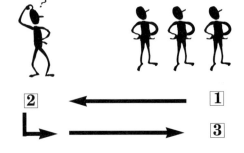

EXTERNALLY REFERENCED THINKING

Those with externally referenced thinking really like to receive feedback and information from other people. In fact, they need feedback from others in order to function effectively, because without it they can feel that they lack focus or direction. At the high preference end of the scale, they may sometimes be perceived as 'blowing with the wind', as they can have a tendency to revise their opinions depending on the feedback they receive from others. This can mistakenly be perceived as being 'weak-minded', particularly by internally referenced thinkers.

Externally referenced thinkers often care deeply about what other people think of them. They can sometimes find it difficult to deal with criticism or negative feedback as they have no internal checks to evaluate its validity. This can, on occasion, be interpreted as lacking in self-confidence.

In their careers they are ideally suited to jobs where other people's opinions matter. They are very diplomatic and make good salespeople as they really listen to what their customers have to say, and are also highly motivated to achieve the sales targets set them.

MANAGEMENT AND MOTIVATION

Externally referenced thinkers are generally 'easy' to manage. They will frequently check back with their managers to ensure that they are doing their job satisfactorily. They also need to be certain that, if they have any problems, they can reach their manager straight away for guidance. A very high score may indicate that they need constant and ongoing feedback, which some managers may find difficult to deal with after a while. (This assumes of course that managers want their staff to be self-sufficient – some may not!)

As managers, externally referenced thinkers are good at following directions from above and implementing the agreed strategy, although they can sometimes find it difficult to make decisions or counter negative feedback from dissenters. They may prefer to follow instructions or guidelines rather than decide for themselves, particularly as they are often able to understand both sides of a debate. They may, therefore, agree with all parties to some extent. This means that decision-making can be awkward for them at times.

EXERCISES

To practise developing your externally referenced thinking skills:

◆ ask for feedback from more than one source
◆ put yourself in another person's position so you can understand more fully how they have arrived at their conclusions
◆ ask people for feedback on your performance or behaviour and act on it rather than dismissing it as not valid

IN SUMMARY

✔	Internal
	➢ have standards within themselves
	➢ self-opinionated, possibly even arrogant
	➢ ignore feedback from others
	➢ may be overconfident
	➢ possess leadership qualities

✔	External
	➤ rely on external input
	➤ swayed by others' opinions
	➤ need feedback from others
	➤ may lack self-confidence
	➤ possess 'followership' qualities

WHAT'S YOUR SCORE?

Now that you have read this chapter you may want to estimate your degree of preference for these thinking styles. Fill in your score below:

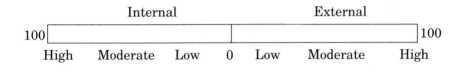

When you have estimated your scores, transfer them to the Summary Profile in Chapter 17.

The advantage of doing one's praising for oneself is that one can lay it on so thick and exactly in the right places.
Samuel Butler

Be wiser than other men, but do not tell them so.
Lord Chesterfield

14 **Self and Others**

There are two types of people – those who come in the room and say, 'Well, here I am!' and those who come in and say, 'Ah, there you are.'

Frederick L. Collins

These thinking styles relate to people's focus of attention and the way in which they respond to their own and other people's needs. Do they focus on themselves or others?

SELF-REFERENCED THINKING

As the name suggests, people with a self-referenced orientation are motivated by their own wants and needs. These people can be very 'self-contained' and for this reason may be perceived as aloof, with little time for other people. This can mean that they enjoy a role where they can work alone as opposed to working within a team, and they are keen on remuneration and performance awards which reflect their individual contribution.

They frequently rise to positions of seniority in organizations because they find it easy to remain focused on their own goals and are not unduly concerned by whom they have to step on in order to achieve those goals. They also have a tendency to surround themselves with a specialist team to support them, and they will sometimes take this team from organization to organization if they make a career move.

'Self' can also indicate a client, team, department or even organizational focus. So 'self' may not mean 'What's in it for me?', but rather, 'What's in it for my client, team?' etc.

A highly self-referenced scoring person could be described as 'selfish' and may be interested in the acquisition of material wealth or status. Often very competitive, self-referenced thinking people can make good leaders in the sense that other people are frequently willing to follow them, knowing that they will be 'looked after'. A low self-score may mean that someone needs to finish what they are doing first, before they can turn their attention to others. Remember that there are some circumstances when it is very important to 'put yourself first', for example, first aid and emergency situations where your own safety is paramount to your ability to help others. In fact, the first rule of first aid is 'ensure your own safety'.

If I am not for myself who is for me?
Rabbi Hillel

COMPETITIVE SPORTS

I have noticed during the course of my research that world class sportsmen and women have a self-orientation when they are competing, including those in team-based sports, where 'self' is likely to mean 'my team'. An Olympic pairs canoeist explained to me that for them, there are a number of reasons for this:

- 'self' means their team and also the canoe club they represent
- rather obviously, putting the 'other' team or team members first would not ensure success
- they want to win for themselves, and value the self-recognition they would gain
- they are extremely focused on the goal that they want to achieve sometimes to the exclusion of everything else, including their friends and family

Remember, though, this is context specific. Both Gary Lineker and Rory Underwood, for example, have a self orientation when playing competitive sports, but in a social setting have an others preference.

MANAGEMENT AND MOTIVATION

Managing self thinkers is easy, provided that you explain what the advantages or benefits would be for 'them'. As they are likely to prefer an autonomous role, focus on their objectives, allowing some flexibility in letting them decide for themselves how best to achieve those goals and reward them for their individual contribution wherever possible.

As managers they will be supportive of any person or idea which they perceive as being useful to them, the department or organization in some way. Highly self-oriented thinkers need to ensure that they take the time to listen to their staff and colleagues and don't become detached, distant or inaccessible. Also, if 'self' for them really does mean 'themselves', they need to take care that their staff don't feel that they are being 'used' or 'taken advantage of'.

EXERCISES
To practise becoming a more self-referenced thinker:
◆ book some time into your diary for yourself and make that time non-negotiable
◆ put yourself and your needs first occasionally
◆ refuse demands for your time unless you are particularly committed to the person who has asked you or the task they have asked you to do

OTHERS REFERENCED THINKING
The focus of attention for others-oriented thinkers is on the wants and needs of other people. They are very good with people and make attentive friends and workmates, doing their best to ensure that their friends and colleagues at work are OK. You can always rely on them to do you a favour.

However, be aware that someone with a high score on the others scale can sometimes give away so much of themselves that they don't leave enough time or energy *for* themselves, which means that they can become permanently exhausted.

Life's most urgent question is:
What are you doing for others?
Martin Luther King, Jr

The ideal job role for an others-focused thinker is one where they are able to interact with other people or where the needs of others are important. Although I have said in the Introduction to this book that the majority of job roles can be fulfilled by any combination of preferences, this is one of the exceptions where I will be prescriptive. If I were in hospital or needed a nurse or a carer of some sort, of the two preferences described in this chapter, I know which preference I would want them to have!

We have recently recruited a new nanny to look after our three-year-old daughter, and although Thinking Styles was designed as a development tool rather than a recruitment instrument, in our household, a prerequisite for a successful appointment is a high others score.

In studies of financial services and car sales, interestingly, others thinkers were the highest performing salespeople. They really listened to what their customers wanted and were highly motivated to satisfy their needs, sometimes even giving up some of their commission in order to secure a better deal for their customers.

MANAGEMENT AND MOTIVATION
Others-preferenced thinkers make good managers because they are very concerned with the well-being of their staff, often taking on a slightly parental role in the management of their team. By this I mean that they protect, support and discipline their team by turn where appropriate. This can sometimes be a weakness, however, as they may avoid

taking decisions or implementing strategies which they believe could have a detrimental effect on others. Supportive managers will be happy for their team to take the credit for any individual or team successes.

When managing others thinkers remember that they will be motivated by being part of a team and by feeling that their contribution is valued. Also, it is often important for them to feel personally valued by both their managers and the other members of the team.

EXERCISES

To practise becoming more others referenced:

◆ put yourself 'in someone else's shoes' in a given situation and imagine what it's like for *them*

◆ listen to what people say and watch their body language

◆ put someone else's needs first, either individually or for a group of people

IN SUMMARY

✔	Self
	➤ put own needs first
	➤ do not notice, or ignore, others' needs
	➤ may be perceived as selfish
	➤ motivated to help by personal gain
	➤ 'self' may mean myself, my client, my team, or my organization

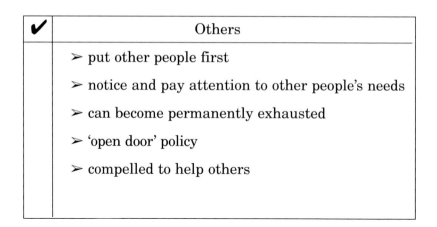

✔	Others
	➤ put other people first
	➤ notice and pay attention to other people's needs
	➤ can become permanently exhausted
	➤ 'open door' policy
	➤ compelled to help others

It is one of the most beautiful compensations of this life
that no man can sincerely try to help another
without helping himself.
Ralph Waldo Emerson

WHAT'S YOUR SCORE?

Now that you have read this chapter you may want to estimate your degree of preference for these thinking styles. Fill in your score below:

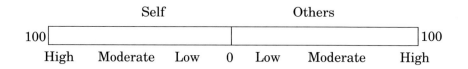

When you have estimated your scores, transfer them to the Summary Profile in Chapter 17.

15   Match and Mismatch

The reasonable man adapts himself to the world;
the unreasonable one persists in trying to adapt the
world to himself. Therefore all progress depends on
the unreasonable man.

George Bernard Shaw

These thinking styles relate to people's automatic response when they are *told* (rather than asked) to do something. Do they comply immediately, or is their immediate response to disagree, asking why they should or even refusing outright?

MATCHING THINKING
Someone with a preference for matching processes through agreement and collaboration. They like to fit in and try to avoid conflict if at all possible because they find disagreement and argument extremely uncomfortable. They are generally flexible people who fit easily into corporate culture and will readily wear the corporate uniform of language and behaviour.

Great discoveries and improvements invariably involve
the co-operation of many minds.
Alexander Graham Bell

They are likely to be good at following instructions, in fact they often quite like to be told what to do. However, they can sometimes find it hard to refuse requests or be assertive where it would be appropriate, preferring to take on more themselves rather than having to say 'No' to someone else.

Matching thinking tends to be traditional rather than radical in its approach and ideas, and can best be described as George Bernard Shaw's 'reasonable man' in the quote on the previous page. I have noticed, though, that matching thinkers can have a tendency to 'subversively mismatch'. By this I mean that, rather than face a direct confrontation, disagreement or even heated discussion, they will agree to a certain course of action and then somehow manage not to implement it.

Those with a mismatching thinking style preference find this behaviour both baffling and frustrating. They would much rather someone disagreed with them to their face and discussed it so that they could, through disagreement, reach agreement. This approach more closely matches their own natural thinking pattern.

MANAGEMENT AND MOTIVATION

Managing those who have a preference for matching thinking is 'easy' because they make good team members and are supportive of their colleagues and managers. Motivate them by shielding them from disagreement or conflict and make sure they know that you value their contribution. If they make a habit of subversively mismatching they are likely to affect their career progression in the long term, however do remember that their intention is to avoid conflict, not to be 'difficult'.

As managers they like to keep the peace and will do their very best to ensure that everyone around them is as happy as they can be given the set of circumstances that prevail at the time. They are very supportive of the people who work for them and with them, although they cannot always be relied upon to fight their corner in confrontational managerial situations. This can lead to a perception of them being weak managers, although I have noticed that effective managers will confront and disagree when appropriate, *even* when it makes them feel uncomfortable.

EXERCISES

To practise your matching thinking:
- align yourself to the other people in a group, in terms of either your beliefs, your language patterns or in the clothes you wear
- match other people's body language and build rapport
- when told to do something, willingly comply at once
- have a conversation or discussion with someone and agree with them throughout

MISMATCHING THINKING

As the name suggests, those with a mismatching thinking style preference are quite happy to do the opposite to everyone else. These are the rebel leaders and revolutionaries who will bend and break rules. They are George Bernard Shaw's 'unreasonable man'. They 'think outside the box' and shift the paradigm by continually questioning and disagreeing with the state of the world around themselves.

We started off trying to set up a small anarchist community, but people wouldn't obey the rules.
Alan Bennett

Mismatching thinkers often have high energy levels and they tend to be high achievers at work because they are prepared to take risks, particularly because their initial response to a situation is to ask both 'Why?' and 'Why not?'

Because their brains process information through disagreement, these thinkers move from 'No' to 'Yes'. This means that they have to disagree with you in order to then agree with you at a later stage. When given instructions the immediate and automatic response of a mismatching referenced person is either to say 'No' or to ask 'Why?' Sometimes this is done internally within their own mind, at other times they speak their mind out loud. They may change their mind and happily comply at a later stage. They are not very good at hiding their true feelings and tend to dislike politics at work, preferring to focus directly on the challenges which face them rather than be distracted by games-playing.

In meetings they will sometimes take on the role of 'devil's advocate' because they think that someone ought to, and not necessarily because they believe the stance they have proposed or are arguing for. Remember, it is the process of disagreement that they are motivated by; they may not necessarily actually disagree with you. It is this behaviour which a matching thinker finds both difficult to comprehend and hard to deal with.

In order to learn, mismatch preferenced people will interrupt, ask questions, disagree with others, and possibly be 'disruptive' or even 'difficult'. This is simply how they process information and they actually *need* to do this in order to be able to absorb and integrate new information effectively. It is not a reflection on their trainer/teacher/facilitator, boss or colleague, in fact it has nothing to do with them or the quality of the information being presented, it is just the way in which a mismatcher's brain works.

WORKING WITH MISMATCHING THINKERS
In my experience, there are two ways to deal effectively with someone with a mismatching preference. The first is to use humour, particularly because they themselves are often 'practical jokers' and much comedy is a 'juxtaposition', i.e. a punchline that you were not expecting.

PHILBERT DECIDED TO LIVEN THINGS UP WITH
ONE OF HIS FAMOUS PRACTICAL JOKES

The second way is to be firm regarding the boundaries of what is acceptable mismatching behaviour and what is not.

Knowing this can make a huge difference to the quality of your relationships, and it is my sincere hope that it will make the lives of many people in organizations profoundly more comfortable.

MANAGEMENT AND MOTIVATION

Managing those with a mismatching thinking style preference can be quite challenging at times because they are likely to continually disagree with you. This can lead to them being described as difficult to manage or mavericks due to their tendency to break the rules. Provided they are asked rather than told what to do, they will have little to rebel against. Therefore asking them to do something will generally elicit a more positive response.

I saw an article in which my old school was quoted as saying that I wasn't expelled. Well I was. I just didn't do anything they wanted me to do. They were the five happiest years of my life. I loved them.

Jeremy Clarkson

As managers they can sometimes be perceived as difficult to approach as they are likely to disagree or challenge an idea or proposal the first time they hear it – even if it is, in reality, a very good idea! However, their staff can rely on them to be supportive and they will fight hard on behalf of someone or something they value or believe in.

EXERCISES

To practise developing your mismatching thinking skills:

- deliberately don't do something that you've told yourself that you 'should' or 'must' do
- play a practical joke on someone who you know won't mind
- role play a disagreement or conflict situation at work

✔	Match
	➢ process through agreement
	➢ 'easy' to manage
	➢ like to 'fit in'
	➢ collaborative approach
	➢ avoid conflict and argument
	➢ start from 'Yes'

✔	Mismatch
	➢ process through disagreement
	➢ 'difficult' to manage
	➢ practical joker
	➢ play 'devil's advocate'
	➢ embrace conflict and argument
	➢ move from 'No' to 'Yes'

WHAT'S YOUR SCORE?

Now that you have read this chapter you may want to estimate your degree of preference for these thinking styles. Fill in your score below:

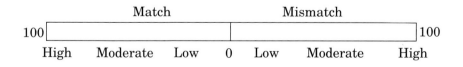

When you have estimated your scores, transfer them to the Summary Profile in Chapter 17.

16 Sameness and Difference

People are very open minded about new things
– as long as they're exactly like the old ones.
Charles Kettering

These thinking styles concern how a person relates to change, and the frequency and magnitude of change that they feel comfortable with.

SAMENESS THINKING

Those with a preference for sameness thinking tend to have a low tolerance for change as they are motivated by stability. They find change acceptable only if it is gradual and not too drastic. They are best described as 'evolutionaries not revolutionaries' who will actively resist change if they perceive it to be too radical or extreme, in which case they are likely to 'dig their heels in' and may refuse to co-operate.

Sameness thinkers are attracted to organizations or industries which they think will offer them a degree of security or stability, and to job roles which offer them the opportunity to make steady progress. They are likely to have been in the same job for a number of years and will only accept major change once every ten years or so. They prefer a role where they can repeat tasks, which makes them ideally suited to administrative, procedural or maintenance activities, or any job in which the day-to-day activities are largely the same.

Because they have a low tolerance for difference, sameness thinkers can be useful in areas such as quality control or quality assurance, where consistency is important. Their low tolerance for difference means that they both notice and reject what is different or does not conform. They are most happy to work on activities or projects where they are continuing to improve or develop something which already exists, rather than working on something from the beginning or initiating something 'new' themselves.

He who is firmly seated in authority soon learns to think
security and not progress.
James Russell Lowell

MANAGEMENT AND MOTIVATION
As managers sameness oriented thinkers do not appreciate surprises, and like consistency in their staff. They value stability highly and do not like mavericks in their teams as a maverick represents too high a degree of difference for them to feel comfortable.

To manage sameness thinkers assign them similar tasks, stressing their similarity to other pre-existing and familiar tasks. Motivate them by identifying ways in which they can progress and develop over time and if you must make changes, introduce them gradually.

EXERCISES
To practise developing your sameness thinking skills:
◆ undertake your workplace maintenance activities at the same time every day
◆ compare two proposals or reports, identifying the similarities between them
◆ develop a project, making gradual improvements to it, while keeping it basically the same

DIFFERENCES THINKING

Someone with a preference for differences thinking has a high tolerance for frequent and major change. They will resist situations and environments which *they* perceive to be static. At the extreme, these people are revolutionaries who support completely new beginnings and who advocate an 'out with the old, in with the new' philosophy. Highly differences oriented thinkers like variety within their jobs and are likely to make a job change every few years or so, even though they may stay within the same organization for much longer.

These are the appropriate people to involve in strategic change programmes, or to have in positions where they can 'turn the business round' and really make a difference to an organization. Have you ever wondered why it is that chief executives, who are often brought in to 'make a difference', seem to stay in their positions for approximately two to three years before they move on?

These may be the appropriate people to have in place to instigate change, however, they may not be the right people to have in place if you want to engender a period of stability in an organization. This is because they can have a tendency to encourage change just because their own personal tolerance for change is so high and they become either bored or frustrated if the degree of change is too slow for *them*. For a period of stability after major change, someone with some flexibility on the sameness scale might be more appropriate.

MANAGEMENT AND MOTIVATION

To manage differences thinkers focus on how the project or task is different from the other things that they have been involved with and give them variety in their jobs if at all possible. Identify what they can learn which is new, or which will differentiate them in the marketplace. Be prepared to listen to them if their opinions differ from your own, and give them the opportunity to 'make a difference' in some way.

As managers these people are often original thinkers who are interesting to work for. However, they can become easily distracted by the latest fad, innovation or new set of circumstances. They will probably be happy to delegate some of the more mundane and repetitive tasks to their staff. They will appreciate a novel approach to problem-solving, and they will also be keen to manage a team recognized as unique or unusual within their organisation or industry.

EXERCISES
To practise developing your differences thinking:
◆ identify some of the ways in which your life or your job are different now compared with five years ago
◆ write down the ways in which you have made a difference to your organization or to the lives of the people you work with
◆ read two proposals or reports identifying areas of difference between them

Let me tell you about the very rich.
They are different from you and me.
F. Scott Fitzgerald to Ernest Hemingway.
Yes, they have more money, replied Hemingway.

✔	Sameness
	➢ low tolerance for change
	➢ value stability
	➢ like to make steady progress
	➢ prefer gradual change
	➢ notice what is similar
	➢ major change every 10 years

✔	Difference
	➢ like radical change
	➢ no need for stability
	➢ become bored when every day is perceived as the same
	➢ notice what is different
	➢ like to make a difference

What's Your Score?

Now that you have read this chapter you may want to estimate your degree of preference for these thinking styles. Fill in your score below:

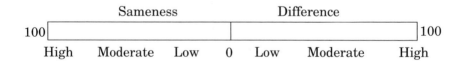

When you have estimated your scores, transfer them to the Summary Profile in Chapter 17.

You will now have completed your Other Criteria Thinking Styles Profile. It is important to remember that there are no 'right' or 'wrong' profiles. What it is true to say, however, is that some thinking styles preferences are more appropriate for some job roles in certain circumstances.

Remember that we can all do things which do not match our natural thinking style, we just may not find them as comfortable or as easy to do.

Statistically, for the computer scored questionnaire there are 17 million possible combinations of individual profile. So it is likely that, even if your profile appears similar to someone else's, in reality it is actually quite different.

More detailed information on understanding your profile and completing the computer scored questionnaire follow in the next few chapters.

Personal and Organizational Development

17 **Completing Your Own Thinking Styles Profile**

SENSORY CRITERIA

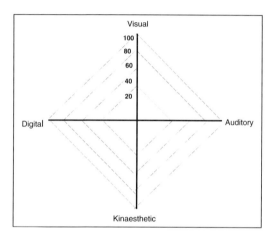

OTHER CRITERIA

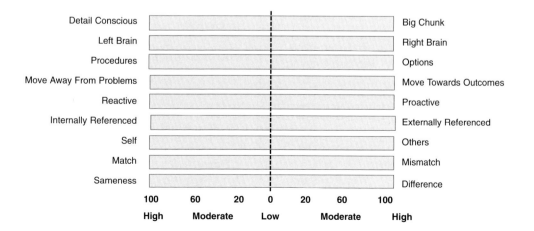

After having read this book, you may want to complete the profile for yourself, or attend one of our Thinking Styles® workshops. Details of the workshops are in Chapter 20.

You will find a copy of the questionnaire and step-by-step instructions on how to complete it on the web site at *www.thinkingstyles.co.uk*. There are 80 questions and it takes about 15 minutes to complete. You can download the questionnaire, complete it off-line and then e-mail it back to us, or you can download it and print it off, fill it in by hand and then fax or post it back to us, whichever is most convenient for you.

Alternatively, if you do not have internet facilities available to you, contact us directly and we will send you a copy of the questionnaire. Our contact details are in Chapter 20. Up-to-date prices are available on request and are also on the web site. Payment can be made either by cheque or credit card. On receipt of both your questionnaire and your payment we will send you the following:

Personal Feedback Individually written for you	Thinking Styles® **Profile Report**
Personal Strengths & Weaknesses Summary	Suggested **Personal Development Plan**

If you are involved in working with teams and are interested in building more cohesive and effective working groups, you might consider using either the Thinking Styles Team Profile (showing the comparison of styles between team members) or the Thinking Styles Two-Way Relationship Profile (showing the comparison of styles of two individuals).

Both of these will help you to understand people's individual thinking style preferences and will enable you to work to strengths and compensate for any potential weaknesses. Respecting and valuing team members' Thinking Styles will build a cohesive and more effective team.

Please contact us if we can be of any assistance.

18 Applications

My intention in this chapter is to identify and give an overview of some of the applications of Thinking Styles. These will be covered in more depth in the second book of the Thinking Styles series, *Case Studies and Applications*.

MANAGING PEOPLE

LEADERSHIP

> *A leader cannot afford to be a good communicator,*
> *he must be a great communicator.*

> William Hodges

What does this actually mean? It means that like Churchill, a leader must understand the impact their words and language have on others. All leadership studies agree on one thing: leadership is all about influencing – the ability to influence in a way that is both acceptable to and accepted by a majority. Understanding your own thinking styles preferences and the language patterns you use because of those preferences will enable you to more fully understand what you are saying. By matching your behaviour to your words, you will gain congruence and credibility, both key leadership qualities.

MANAGEMENT DEVELOPMENT

One of the main attributes of truly effective managers is their flexible approach to the people they manage. Some people are easier to manage than others, which by definition, makes other people more 'difficult'. This is just as true for bosses – some are easier to work for than others!

Understanding more about yourself and other people will not only make you more effective at managing your team, it will make you a more effective boss as well. I strongly believe that in the next century one of the most important managerial competencies will be cognitive flexibility, which Thinking Styles identifies and develops.

TEAMWORKING

Have you ever been part of a team that hasn't worked? A team where perhaps the contingency planning wasn't done or where no one paid enough attention to the important details. Even worse than these examples is a team where personal in-fighting and a lack of respect for individual team members ensure that the team never truly performs. Understanding individuals' thinking styles preferences will enable you to work to people's cognitive strengths and compensate for any potential weaknesses where the team's cognitive flexibility is poor, or where the team is unbalanced. Respecting and valuing individual's thinking styles and processing patterns will help build a cohesive and more effective working team.

RELATIONSHIP MARKETING

MARKETING

Successful marketing materials are written using the specific words and language patterns which will attract their target market. To understand what I mean more fully, do the following exercise: Collect examples of those marketing materials which appeal to you and those which don't. Pick out the words or phrases which you either find attractive or which put you off buying the product or service. Next match the words with your thinking styles preferences. You will discover a significant correlation between these two sets of information.

SALES NEGOTIATIONS

Most sales directors will agree that it is the ability of their sales force to build rapport with their customers and potential customers which is their most valuable skill. Understanding the thinking styles preferences and associated language patterns will help you develop rapport quickly and easily. If you are involved in merger or acquisition negotiations, the ability to develop rapport quickly, understand the other team's cognitive preferences and present information to them in ways that match those preferences will give any negotiating team a significant advantage.

CUSTOMER SERVICE

Effective customer service, particularly from call centres, has been one of the most complex human resources issues of the last decade. Spending considerable lengths of time sitting still and talking to customers one cannot see face to face will be difficult for all but those with high auditory or auditory visual flexibility.

I have also noticed that, apart from their ability to develop rapport quickly and professionally, good customer service executives are also able to follow company procedures while at the same time maintaining a balance of internal and external focus. Of course this does oversimplify the role somewhat. Suffice it to say that by using thinking styles to benchmark those people who perform outstandingly and comparing them to those who don't, you will be able to model excellent performance in the role and reduce staff turnover in the longer term as people will be better able to understand the competencies they need to develop for excellent performance.

EFFECTIVENESS AT WORK

EFFECTIVE MEETINGS

What is an effective meeting? We all have our own opinions. However, all meetings will benefit from pre-planning and paying attention to the preferred thinking styles of attendees. This will maintain focus on the outcome of the meeting and avoid potential conflict often caused by misunderstanding colleagues' language preferences.

(A short case study on effective meetings is included in Chapter 19.)

PROJECT MANAGEMENT

Project managers require a unique combination of skills and flexibility. They are required to juggle the tasks and priorities of the project in both overview and detail; to maintain a positive (towards) focus while also contingency planning (away from); to have the interpersonal skills required to manage their project team *and* the tactical skills necessary to manage their client. Although the knowledge required by project managers has been quantifiable and measurable for some time, Thinking Styles now offers a unique opportunity to identify and measure the cognitive preferences and flexibility which the best project managers employ.

TRAINING AND CONSULTANCY

LEARNING

How we learn most easily and the flexibility we have regarding our learning style will be closely related to our thinking styles. The best teachers have known for a long time that children learn in different ways. This is becoming even more important as we are beginning to understand that people with dyslexia for example learn differently because they think differently. The thinking comes first. For example, many children learn by 'doing'. This is a kinaesthetic learning style which involves movement and action. It is a shame that within the National Curriculum, physical education activity is now becoming limited to make way for literacy and numeracy projects. I believe that, paradoxically, by increasing exercise in a focused way, particularly if Accelerated Learning techniques are included, we could actually increase and improve literacy and numeracy skills in school children.

(This subject will be covered in more depth in *Thinking Styles in Education*, the third book in the Thinking Styles series which will be available in 2001.)

TRAINING

It never occurred to me until I became interested in understanding thinking styles that the way I plan, structure, deliver and evaluate training programmes, either for groups or one-to-one coaching, would be a direct reflection of my own thinking style preferences.

So what would be the 'best' or 'ideal' thinking styles profile for a trainer? In a way there is no 'ideal' profile, as all preferences have their advantages and disadvantages for the training and learning of others. Also, within certain cultures and environments, some preferences are more appropriate than others. For example, where either logic or creativity are highly valued, a trainer with the cognitive flexibility to match the culture would be more suitable.

Developing flexibility and exploring which training methods best suit each thinking style preference is an area we cover in depth in our workshop 'Thinking Styles for Trainers'.

As a consultant myself, I mostly tend to work with either other consultants or clients. Even my own colleagues are, by definition, consultants. My company has a number of strategic partnerships with other consultancies and we have found the process of understanding each other's thinking style preferences invaluable in terms of being able to comprehend and respects others' ways of working. Thinking styles has given us a common language. For larger consultancies, where teams come together and need to 'get up to speed' quickly, thinking styles has proved most beneficial.

Understanding our clients' cognitive preferences, enables us to do a number of things better:
• develop rapport and build relationships
• hold more effective meetings
• present proposals and write reports more clearly than we did before

We have also found thinking styles very helpful in terms of identifying client culture, which means that we are able to match our consultants with the prevailing culture and avoid any potential mismatches.

19 Case study examples

Here are a few examples of how Thinking Styles can be used in a business environment and some of the latest research relating to thinking skills.

GREAT LEADERS – NEW RESEARCH

A recent study by the Cranfield School of Management examined the elements of good leadership. It interviewed over 6,500 senior and middle managers from 14 countries over a 10-year period. Among other things, the research found that:

Eighty per cent of the most effective leaders combine two traits – being good at both strategy and day-to-day operational management. The most accomplished leaders are strategists with an eye for managing detail.

In thinking styles terms, that means that they have a big chunk preference, with the flexibility to move across into detail conscious where necessary. An interesting benchmark for both current and aspiring leaders.

MANAGERS' SKILLS FOR THE NEW MILLENNIUM

Recent independent research by one of the major UK business schools has identified a number of skills prerequisite for managerial success in the next century. Among them 'cognitive' thinking skills rates highly on the list. Good news for clients using Thinking Styles in their management development programmes.

MEETING TIMES HALVED

British Aerospace Regional Aircraft, Woodford site, have halved the time of their weekly production meeting from three hours down to one and a half. The ten senior managers who attend the meeting are delighted with the progress they have made since being profiled using Thinking Styles.

Internal Consultant Irene Foxley tells us that it is because they are much more focused. They describe themselves as 'sharper', and because they understand each other's profiles, arguments have been reduced and they feel that their relationships and communication skills have improved.

Instead of cutting the meeting time in half, the team have decided to 'build more into the meeting. A situation we are all more than happy with'. Early calculations as to the bottom line benefits for the organization are estimated to be in the region of £25,000 per annum.

IMPROVED RELATIONSHIPS AND BETTER TEAMWORK

Dwilla Mortimore, an experienced management consultant and executive coach at director level, identified a problem which was causing her a lot of discomfort at work. Over the years she had reached an uneasy truce with her boss. Both experienced managers, Dwilla said, 'I'm too old to be told what to do.'

Our solution was to profile them both and generate a Two-Way Relationship Profile so they could more easily identify each other's strengths and potential weaknesses. Dwilla described it as:

*a breakthrough – we discovered that we are too alike –
we're both Internally Referenced Mismatchers which
means that we both think that we know best, and we are
prepared to argue about it. So that's what we used to do
all the time – argue. Now that we've had our Thinking
Styles Profile done together we get on better than we have
in twenty years. It just goes to show that you're never too
old to learn something new.*

Dwilla is a very youthful 64 and in such demand that her
clients won't let her retire!

20 Workshops

We currently run four types of workshops at regular intervals throughout the year. These workshops are available as both public programmes and bespoke in-house programmes. As Thinking Styles can be a difficult area to grasp due to its complexity, Accelerated Learning techniques are built into the design of the workshops to make your learning both easy and fun.

INTRODUCTION TO THINKING STYLES   (One-day workshop)
This workshop is designed to familiarize you with Thinking Styles in more detail than we have been able to do in this book.

The day includes:

- a presentation on the Thinking Styles criteria
- your own personal Thinking Styles Profile and Report
- personal feedback on your profile
- discussion groups on the implications of your profile, for yourself and others
- group presentations on the applications of Thinking Styles for yourself and your organization
- lunch and all refreshments
- the opportunity to network

FACILITATOR TRAINING AND LICENSING   (Two-day workshop)
This workshop is designed for those people who want to become trained and licensed to use Thinking Styles and give feedback to others using Thinking Styles.

The two days include all of the inputs and outputs of the Introductory Workshop, plus:

- a much greater understanding of the implications of your own Thinking Styles preferences and flexibility
- group discussions on the strengths and potential weaknesses of each criterion
- practice at giving feedback to others using Thinking Styles
- case study examples
- presentation skills development using Thinking Styles
- an exploration of Accelerated Learning techniques

THINKING STYLES FOR TRAINERS   (One-day workshop)
This workshop is specifically designed for experienced trainers to further develop their existing skills. Participants will:

- learn advanced communication skills
- learn which training methods best suit each thinking preference
- learn Accelerated Learning techniques
- learn how to build Accelerated Learning techniques into their own training programmes
- improve their effectiveness as trainers

THINKING STYLES AND TEAMWORK   (One-day workshop)

This workshop is designed for either new or existing teams to help them understand and exploit their cognitive strengths and develop individual and team flexibility. They will:

- understand and value differences in thinking style
- understand where similarity in thinking styles is valuable
- understand the critical cognitive success factors for high performance teams
- understand how to assign tasks and responsibilities to match people's cognitive strengths
- encourage and develop flexibility within the team
- learn how to recognize individual and team strengths and weaknesses more easily
- be able to identify which teams will 'work' and which won't, and why
- learn how to build high-performance teams

Future dates and booking details for public courses are available on the web site or on request.

BJA Associates also offer consultancy and bespoke training on Teambuilding and Advanced Communication Skills for management teams and senior executives at board level.

Please contact us if we can be of assistance.

See contact details over the page.

BJA Associates Ltd
Stainby
Grantham
Lincolnshire
NG33 5QT

Telephone: 01476 861010 (UK)
                    +44 1476 861010 (outside UK)

Fax: 01476 861645 (UK)
                    +44 1476 861645 (outside UK)

Web site: *http://www.thinkingstyles.co.uk*
E-mail: *info@thinkingstyles.co.uk*

21 Thinking Styles in Education* Charitable Trust

As well as being the author of Thinking Styles® I am also Founding Trustee of Thinking Styles in Education*. While writing Thinking Styles for business, I recognized how useful a tool it could be in the field of education: for parents, teachers and particularly for the children themselves.

It will be useful for teachers because it will enable them to recognize and understand their own personal thinking preferences. This will affect the ways in which they prefer to structure and deliver their teaching, both in terms of the National Curriculum and any other teaching or learning activities they are involved with.

Also, by recognizing the thinking preferences of children, teachers will be able to teach to a pupil's thinking styles strengths, encourage flexibility and put strategies in place to compensate for any potential weakness in thinking, for all ages of student. Working within existing parameters, Thinking Styles could even be incorporated into the assessment criteria for children in schools.

It seems to me that all parents want the best education for their children. By helping their children recognize and understand how their brains work and become more flexible in their thinking (through the use of laughter, fun, games and lots of physical movement), parents will, as a natural consequence, learn more about themselves and how they think.

All children, even the most 'difficult', like to learn about themselves because they find themselves fascinating. Whole brain thinking and flexibility in both thinking and learning styles will enable children (and adults) to learn more quickly, solve problems more effectively and be more 'intelligent'.

The new source of wealth is intelligence . . . It's the brains and skills of people. . . Everyone has got to get intelligent – in its widest sense.
Professor Charles Handy

Lester Thurow, an American expert on world economic issues, says, 'the dominant competitive weapon of the twenty-first century will be the education and skills of the workforce'. And I will add to his quote by asking, what are our children, if they are not our future?

The stated Objectives of the Trust are:

TO ACT AS A CENTRE FOR INFORMATION AND IDEAS ON, AND TO COLLECT ALL AVAILABLE DATA RELATING TO, THINKING STYLES IN EDUCATION, AND INCLUDING THOSE MATERIALS RELEVANT TO BRAIN RESEARCH THEORIES AND ACCELERATED LEARNING PRINCIPLES AS THEY RELATE TO THINKING AND LEARNING PROCESSES FOR BOTH ADULTS AND CHILDREN, AND TO MAKE THIS KNOWLEDGE READILY AVAILABLE TO ALL INTERESTED PERSONS BY ADVICE AND OTHERWISE

This has become a more user-friendly vision:

To facilitate greater understanding of individual's thinking and learning processes to raise standards so that Britain will be at the forefront of a global economy.

Thinking Styles in Education can be contacted at the following address:

Thinking Styles in Education,
The Old Blue Dog,
Stainby,
Grantham,
Lincolnshire,
NG33 5QT.

Telephone: 01476 861010
Facsimile: 01476 861645

E-mail: charity@thinkingstyles.co.uk

* Thinking Styles in Education has applied to the Charity Commission of England and Wales for Registered status.

22 Recommended Web Sites and Book List

WEB SITES ON LEARNING

http://www.cainelearning.com – the web site of a major US learning company

http://www.funderstanding.com – hosts a forum on the latest research in learning

http://www.jlcbrain.com – Eric Jensen's web site, a US-based educationalist at the forefront of learning

http://www.anglo-american.co.uk – AA Books, a UK site for books on accelerated learning and NLP

http://www.accelerated-learning.com – a US site for books on Accelerated Learning

http://www.seal.org.uk – the web site of the UK-based Society for Effective and Affective Learning

WEB SITES ON NLP

http://www.nlp.com – the web site for the Society of Neuro-Linguistic Programming based in the US

http://www.anlp.org – the UK web site of the Association of NLP'ers

http://www.stant-1.demon.co.uk – Simon Stanton's site, which has many links to other NLP web sites

*All web site addresses correct at time of going to press.

BOOKS

The following short list is just a very small selection of books on the developments in, and applications of, NLP. They can all be bought through AA Books on 01267 211886 or via their web site *www.anglo-american.co.uk*.

The Structure of Magic, Richard Bandler and John Grinder

Strategies of Genius, Robert Dilts

NLP at Work and *NLP Solutions,* Sue Knight

Influencing with Integrity, Genie Laborde

Principles of NLP and *Practical NLP for Managers,* Ian McDermott and Joseph O'Connor

Introduction to NLP, Joseph O'Connor and John Seymour

Sporting Excellence, Ted Garratt